W9-BIS-567

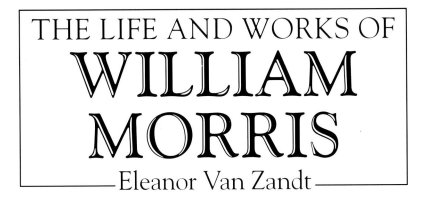

THE LIFE AND WORKS OF
WILLIAM MORRIS

Eleanor Van Zandt

A Compilation of Works from the

BRIDGEMAN ART LIBRARY

The Life and Works of William Morris

This edition printed for:
Shooting Star Press Inc.
230 Fifth Avenue – Suite 1212
New York, NY 10001

Shooting Star Press books are available at special discounts for bulk purchases for sales promotions, premiums, fund-raising, or educational use. Special edition or book excerpts can also be created to specification. For details contact: Special Sales Director, Shooting Star Press Inc., 230 Fifth Avenue, Suite 1212, New York, NY 10001

ISBN 1-57335-034-6

Printed in Italy

Editors:	Barbara Horn, Alexa Stace, Alison Stace, Tucker Slingsby Ltd and Jennifer Warner
Designers:	Robert Mathias • Pedro Prá-Lopez, Kingfisher Design Services
Typesetting/DTP:	Frances Prá-Lopez, Kingfisher Design Services
Picture Research:	Kathy Lockley

The publishers would like to thank Joanna Hartley at the Bridgeman Art Library for her invaluable help.

William Morris   1834-96

William Morris was born into a prosperous middle-class family, and grew up in a fine Georgian mansion in Essex, set in 50 acres of parkland with an adjoining farm. As a boy he spent hours exploring the estate and learning to know and love its profusion of plant life. He also immersed himself in medieval history and legend. These two themes, nature and the Middle Ages, were to dominate his entire creative output.

When he first went to Oxford as a student in 1853, Morris's intention was to enter the Church. The new Anglo-Catholic movement, with its return to pre-Reformation traditions and a corresponding reverence for medieval art and architecture, held a strong appeal for him – as it did for Edward Burne-Jones, who was to become one of the most famous painters of the day and Morris's lifelong friend. Together they also discovered the writings of the art critic and reformer William Ruskin. Abandoning their plans for the priesthood, they determined to lead a crusade against both the vulgar taste of the age and its social injustices.

After leaving university Morris spent the years between 1856 and 1861 pursuing one artistic calling after another, with mixed success. He first began training as an architect in the firm of George Street, where he met Philip Webb, who was to be another close friend. Through Burne-Jones he also met Dante Gabriel Rossetti and other Pre-Raphaelite painters. Encouraged by Rossetti, Morris turned from architecture to painting. At the same time he was writing poetry. His first published collection of poems, *In Defence of Guenevere* (1858), was coldly received by most critics, but later,

Morris would find both his voice as a poet and an enthusiastic public; indeed he was better known in his day as a poet than an artist.

In 1859 Morris got married. His bride, Jane Burden, was the archetypal Pre-Raphaelite beauty, with brooding eyes, a sensuous mouth and thick black hair. She appears in several of Rossetti's paintings and one by Morris himself. Early in their marriage the couple moved into Red House, in Bexleyheath, Kent, which had been designed for them by Philip Webb. Here the Morrises and their friends enjoyed many good times; here their two daughters were born; and here, in 1861, 'the Firm' was conceived.

Originally called Morris, Marshall, Faulkner and Co. (later just Morris and Co.), the Firm was dedicated to raising the standards of craftsmanship and design. By the late 1860s it was receiving important commissions for stained glass in various churches and for designing rooms in various public buildings; one notable commission was for a dining room in the new South Kensington Museum (now the Victoria and Albert) in London.

In addition to such major projects, the Firm produced individual pieces of furniture, wallpaper designs and textiles. In the latter two categories Morris himself took the leading part, and it is for his achievement in these areas that he is best known today. He learned the techniques of the arts for which he designed, so as to understand their fundamental nature. Disliking the harsh synthetic dyes then in use, he studied and experimented with natural dyes in order to produce textiles with the rich, subtle colours of earlier times. He spent many hours examining textiles from other cultures and incorporated some of their characteristics in his own work. 'Follow nature' he advised young designers; 'study antiquity, make your own art.'

Morris was not content only to create; he also worked to educate the public in the importance of good design. 'Have nothing in your houses that you do not know to be useful, or believe to be beautiful.'

This quotation from one of his lectures was Morris's golden rule, and it encapsulates the aims of the Arts and Crafts Movement, of which he was an early leader.

For a few years around 1870 Morris's marriage was badly shaken by a tempestuous relationship between his wife and Rossetti, which ended with Rossetti's decline into mental illness. Morris endured this trial with a patient and generous spirit, even remaining friends with Rossetti, and found comfort in work and travel.

While continuing to work as a designer and businessman, and also as a political activist for the socialist cause, he also managed to write: poetry, prose romances and a Utopian fantasy, *News from Nowhere* (1891). In 1890 he founded The Kelmscott Press, for which he designed some of the typefaces.

By now, ill health was forcing Morris to moderate his prodigious activity. His life with Jane had settled into affectionate companionship, and he had the satisfaction of seeing his daughter May developing into a talented and innovative textile designer. After his death, in 1896, the firm of Morris and Co. continued to prosper, well into the 20th century. Some of Morris's textile and wallpaper designs are still being produced today, and his reputation as one of the great names in the history of design is secure.

Detail

▷ **La Belle Iseult** 1859

Oil on canvas

SOMETIMES CALLED *Queen Guenevere*, this is a portrait of Jane Burden which Morris painted shortly before their marriage. The clue to its identification is the little dog curled up on the bed, who figures in the story of the doomed lovers Tristan and Isolde. In depicting his betrothed as an unfaithful wife, Morris foretold, if unconsciously, the unhappy events that afflicted his and Jane's marriage in later years, when the poet and painter Dante Gabriel Rossetti tried to woo her away from Morris. Although Jane seems to have been touched by the intensity of Rossetti's passion, it is not known whether or not they were lovers. However, she once confided to a friend that she had never loved Morris. The poignancy of this painting is enhanced by the awkwardness with which Jane has been painted – so unlike Rossetti's masterly portraits of her. Morris laboured over the work and at one point wrote plaintively on the canvas, 'I cannot paint you but I love you.'

Detail

▷ **Trellis** c1864

Wallpaper

BY THE TIME Morris began designing wallpapers in the early 1860s, the mid-Victorian taste for elaborate three-dimensional papers was waning. Thanks largely to A.W.N. Pugin, whose wallpapers for the Houses of Parliament had caught the public eye, and to Owen Jones, whose influential book *The Grammar of Ornament* was published in 1856, the fashion was now for flat, stylized geometric motifs, similar to those found in medieval tiles and the borders of stained glass windows. Although a staunch advocate of flat pattern, Morris showed, in his early wallpaper designs, a clear preference for realistically rendered natural forms. This is evident in *Trellis*, which is said to have been inspired by a rose trellis in the courtyard of Red House. The birds and insects in this fresh, unsophisticated design were drawn by Philip Webb.

Detail

◁ **Daisy** 1864

Wallpaper

THE INSPIRATION for this early wallpaper design was an illumination in a medieval manuscript of the works of the French historian and poet Jean Froissart that Morris found in the British Museum. The design was originally used for an embroidered hanging and later for some painted tiles (an important part of the Firm's early output) before being launched as a wallpaper. The naïve, naturalistic treatment of the flowers, which are presented as flat as possible and arranged as if lined up for a group photograph, is in striking contrast to the sophistication of Morris's later wallpaper designs, in which, while adhering to the principle of flat pattern, he sets up wonderfully complex rhythms and a subtle interplay between background and foreground. Although, like Morris's other early wallpapers, *Daisy* was not immediately successful, it gained in popularity as the years passed, and sold well until the beginning of the 20th century.

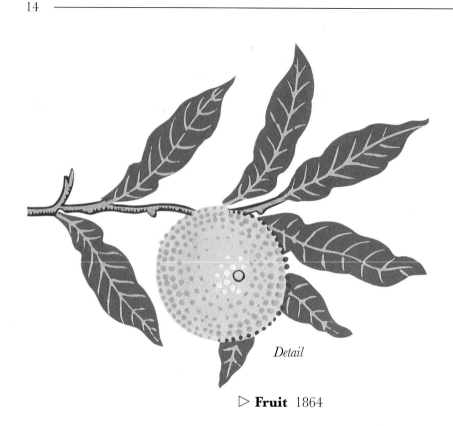

Detail

▷ **Fruit** 1864

Wallpaper

THE STRUCTURE OF *Fruit*, in contrast to that of *Trellis* and *Daisy* (pages 10 and 13 respectively), is not readily perceived. (For the true effect, see pages 16–17). Here, too, the effect is one of charming naturalism; these lemons, oranges, pomegranates and peaches are softly shaped with speckled dots to create an illusion of roundness against an otherwise resolutely flat pattern. Like Morris's other early papers, *Fruit* did not sell well at first, and it was not until 1872 that Morris again turned his hand to wallpaper design. However, the realistic quality of these designs did win some admirers. One customer, a London tradesman, observed proudly to a visitor that the flora on the walls of the room in which they sat seemed 'as if it was all a-growing'.

▷ Morris styles of the 1860s

A NUMBER OF IMPORTANT
furnishings associated with
William Morris are shown as they
were assembled in a temporary
display in London's Victoria and
Albert Museum. They exemplify
the main themes that informed
the work of Morris and his friends:
good craftsmanship, medieval
legend and nature. The large
wardrobe on the left was a
wedding present for the Morrises,
designed by Philip Webb and
Edward Burne-Jones. The
inscription on its left-hand side is
taken from 'The Prioress's Tale' in
Chaucer's *Canterbury Tales*, and the
front of the piece is painted with a
scene from this story. Opposite it
stands the St George Cabinet,
designed by Webb and painted by
Morris with scenes from the story
of how the saint rescued the
princess. The tile overmantel
above the cabinet depicts the story
of 'Sleeping Beauty'. The
adjustable chair in the right-hand
corner is upholstered in Morris's
fabric *Bird* (page 60). The table
has the simple, sturdy character
that would become a hallmark of
the mature Arts and Crafts style.
The settle behind it shows
Morris's love of pattern in its
painted decoration.

▷ **Beauty and the Beast**
c1862

Painted tiles

THIS SEQUENCE OF HAND-
PAINTED tiles was designed by
Morris; the figures were painted
by Burne-Jones. It is similar in
design – including the blue-and-
white patterned background – to
the *Sleeping Beauty* tiles shown on
page 17 and was probably
intended to be placed over a
mantel. Tiles were among the
first items produced by Morris,
Marshall, Faulkner and Co. in
the 1860s. Curiously, in view of
his fascination with the Middle
Ages, Morris showed little interest
in the craft of making medieval-
style encaustic tiles, which were
then enjoying a revival and
enriching the floors of many
English churches. Morris's tiles
were not suitable for use on
floors, or even in fireplaces
(another Victorian fashion); they
were purely decorative objects,
designed to be displayed on walls.
The amount of hand work
involved made them quite
expensive, and few were
produced by the company in later
years. The trellis design that
appears in three of the scenes for
Beauty and the Beast (four including
the dream inset) is similar to that
in *Trellis* (page 10).

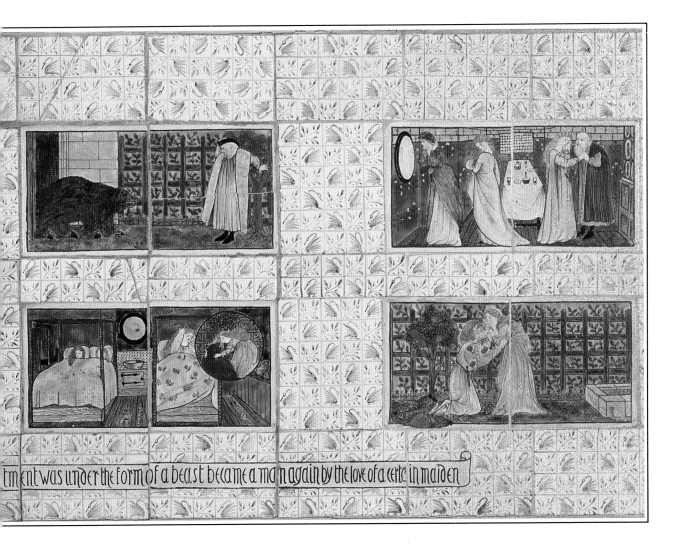

tment was under the form of a beast became a man again by the love of a certe in maiden

Detail

◁ **Saint Catherine** (*detail*) c1865

Embroidery applied to fabric

MORRIS'S INTEREST IN EMBROIDERY dates from his apprenticeship to the architect G.E. Street, who was also an authority on medieval embroidered textiles. Beginning in 1857 – true to his conviction that in order to design for a technique one must have a thorough understanding of it – Morris taught himself to embroider. Many of his early designs were based on religious themes and inspired by medieval English embroidery, *opus anglicanum*. This figure of Saint Catherine is taken from a group of three panels designed for Red House and worked by Jane Morris, a skilled embroiderer. It has been applied to a velvet curtain, together with an accompanying fruit tree bearing a representation of the wheel on which the saint was martyred.

▷ **The Morris Room,
Victoria and Albert Museum**
1868

Interior design

One of the most important
commissions obtained by Morris's
firm in its early years was that of
designing a dining room for the
new South Kensington Museum
of Science and Art (now the
Victoria and Albert Museum). As
the repository of the best examples
of decorative arts, the museum
would later serve as a major
source of inspiration for Morris's
textile designs, and it was
extremely apt that its trustees
should choose his firm – soon to
be the leading name in British
design – to decorate this
important room. Originally called
the Green Dining Room, it
survives more or less intact in the
museum today. 'Dark' and 'rich'
are the adjectives that spring to
mind in describing it. Morris and
his friends gave free rein here to
their love of medieval splendour.
The deep green walls, painted in
relief; the stained glass set in late-
medieval-style casement windows
and painted decorative panels
(both by Burne-Jones); and the
frieze depicting dogs chasing hares
(by Webb) all combine to produce
an effect of high drama.

◁ **Angel with a Rebec** (*detail*)
c1870

Stained glass

THIS WINDOW IS ONE OF A GROUP
of three lancets in the Church of
St Michael, Tilehurst, Berkshire.
In these windows the figures are
by Morris himself, and their richly
embellished gowns display his
delight in pattern. The design and
making of stained glass windows
constituted an important part of
the business of Morris's company
from its founding in 1861. The
Gothic revival initiated by Pugin
and others had created a great
demand for stained glass – both
for new churches and for medieval
churches whose glass had been
destroyed by Protestant extremists
during the 16th and 17th
centuries. The craft had fallen into
decline, and by the end of the 18th
century it consisted almost entirely
of painting with enamels on
uncoloured glass. In the windows
produced by Morris and some of
his contemporaries the early
medieval technique of fixing small
pieces of coloured glass (called 'pot
metal') with leading was revived,
while the later technique of
staining with enamel was refined.

◁ **Angel with a violin** (*detail*)
c1870

Stained glass

IN THIS DETAIL from the Tilehurst windows (see opposite) the intense red and blue, typical of early medieval glass, serve as a foil for the dazzling stars and the sumptuous gold-patterned robe of the angel. In most of the Firm's glass commissions the drawing of the figures was done by other artists, such as Burne-Jones, Rossetti and Ford Madox Brown; but the colouring and the pattern of the leading were normally determined by Morris.

◁ **Two angels** c1865-70

Design for stained glass

THESE CHARMING ANGELS, possibly designed to fit on either side of a vault rib above a larger window, show the Morris style at its freshest and most inventive. Note in particular the subtle striation of the wings, the graceful patterning in the top of each light and the sensitive drawing of the faces. Stained glass was not, of course, confined to churches in the Victorian period; it is found also in many houses of the time, especially in hallways, where its rich colouring enlivens some otherwise dark corners.

◁ **Saint Michael** c1872
Stained glass

THIS WINDOW IN THE CHANCEL of St Michael's Church, in the village of Waterford, Hertfordshire, is one of many designed and made by Morris's company for this church. St Michael, as prince of all the angels, is always depicted with wings – here coloured a deep blood-red to form a contrast with his halo and gleaming medieval-style armour. He stands on delicately patterned emerald-green vegetation. The great increase in church-building in Victorian England was a boon to the Firm, providing it with several important commissions during its first decade of existence. St Michael's, Hertfordshire, completed in 1872, was one of these, but fine examples of Morris stained glass can be found all over England. Although Morris and Co. continued to produce glass in later years, the quality declined somewhat, especially after the move to Merton Abbey, when Morris – now concentrating on textiles – no longer oversaw the production of the glass.

Detail

▷ **Jasmine** 1872

Wallpaper

DURING THE 1870s Morris produced some of his finest papers. *Jasmine* is one of the first of this group. It has the fresh, naturalistic quality of the earlier designs, but here the flowers and leaves are handled with much greater assurance in the structure, so that the eye is led over the pattern without coming to rest at any point. Like his printed cottons, Morris's wallpapers were hand block printed. In machine printing the colours used had to be quick-drying. These colours were thin and tended to fade quickly. With block printing, thicker, more stable colours could be used, and each allowed to dry before the next was applied. This time-consuming process made the papers relatively expensive.

Detail

▷ **Powdered 1874**

Wallpaper (printed fabric 1902)

LIKE JASMINE (page 28), this gentle design retains the naïveté of Morris's early wallpaper designs. Here too, however, the motifs are more closely integrated with the background than in *Daisy* (page 13), for example, and more rhythmically arranged over the surface. In the later 1800s it was common for several papers to be used on a wall: one at dado level, one for the main part of the wall, and yet another – perhaps a frieze – near the ceiling. These would be separated by narrow border papers or architectural mouldings. A small pattern such as *Powdered* might be used as part of such a scheme to contrast with a more boldly patterned paper. By the turn of the century small patterns were becoming increasingly popular for fabrics as well as wallpapers, and in 1902 Morris and Co. began to produce *Powdered* as a chintz.

Detail

▷ **Acanthus** 1875

Wallpaper

THIS SUMPTUOUS PATTERN, which might be dubbed 'the apotheosis of the acanthus leaf', has something of the quality of relief sculpture. The gracefully swirling leaves offer a tactile appeal while at the same time being a superb example of flat pattern. 'Do not be afraid of large patterns,' advised Morris in a lecture in 1888. 'If properly designed they are more restful to the eye than small ones…very small rooms, as well as very large rooms look better ornamented with large patterns.' Ironically, in view of Morris's superb wallpaper designs, he used few wallpapers in his own homes. He preferred walls either white-washed or covered with fabric. He sometimes filled the walls from picture rail to skirting with softly pleated printed cottons. In the drawing room of Kelmscott House in Hammersmith, London, where he lived from 1875 onwards, the walls were covered with his *Bird* woven fabric (page 60), hung flat from the picture rail.

Detail

▷ **Acanthus** 1875

Wallpaper

IN THIS DIFFERENT COLOURWAY the main vertical garland of leaves stands out more clearly against the rest of the design. The shading of the foliage is achieved not with solid tones, but instead with feathery hatching, as in stained glass, which follows the graceful outlines. The tiny flowers in the background give it depth and prevent too strong a contrast.

Detail

▷ **Tulip** 1875

Printed fabric

ALONG WITH HIS WALLPAPERS, Morris's printed cottons are today his best-known creations. Yet it was not until the mid-1870s that his company began producing these successfully. Morris worked in collaboration with Thomas Wardle, a Staffordshire silk dyer, who shared his enthusiasm for vegetable dyes and the traditional block printing method. This time-consuming process, which had in recent years been almost totally supplanted by roller printing, was what Morris needed in order to achieve the high quality of design he demanded. *Tulip* is one of Morris's and Wardle's early successes. With its gracefully swaying blooms, this design is one of Morris's most ingratiating.

Detail

▷ **Marigold** 1875

Printed fabric and wallpaper

THIS DENSELY DETAILED PATTERN illustrates the visual interest that Morris could achieve using a single colour. The deep blue shown here was produced using indigo, one of the most problematical natural dyes and one that Morris especially prized for its rich, intense colour. The contrast of dark blue and scarlet was a favourite Morris colour scheme, appearing often in his work in various media. It was not possible to print indigo dye onto the fabric, as one could with other dyes, because it would oxidize on the blocks (turning from the original green to the desired blue) before the blocks could be applied to the fabric. One way of solving this problem was to print the fabric first with a resist on all the areas where blue was not required, and then immerse the cloth into the blue dye vat. Wishing as always to understand the process for which he was designing, Morris went up to Wardle's dye works and did some of the work himself.

Detail

▷ **Marigold** 1875

Printed fabric and wallpaper

IN THIS ALTERNATIVE COLOURWAY the actual colour of marigold flowers is used, producing a softer, warmer effect. Several different plants could be used to produce a yellow dye, but they were all somewhat fugitive and had to be fixed with a solution of bran in order to be made permanent. Many of Morris and Co.'s fabric designs, such as this one, were also used for wallpaper. The blocks used for the papers were acquired in this century by Arthur Sanderson and Sons Ltd, who continue to produce hand printed papers from them, as well as a select range of machine-printed papers and fabrics.

◁ **Artichoke** c1875

Original design

AT THE TIME MORRIS produced this design he was also producing his first block-printed cottons, in collaboration with Thomas Wardle, of Leek, Staffordshire. Like these printed textiles, *Artichoke* reflects his mastery of repeating patterns. Morris's embroideries of this period also show the influence of woven textiles from Turkey and Persia and of English 17th century crewel embroidery – this last is evident in the large, richly shaded leaves. In order to obtain colours of the required depth and subtlety he used wool and silk threads dyed with natural dyes by Wardle's firm and, later, by his own dye works at Merton Abbey, Surrey.

▷ **Artichoke** 1877

Embroidered wall hanging

THIS IS ONE OF A SET of hangings commissioned by Ada Godman as furnishings for her home. It was worked by Mrs Godman herself, using crewel wools on linen fabric. The stitches include some of Morris's favourites: long and short (in the shaded foliage), satin (stems and small petals) and stem (the outlines). These flat stitches lent themselves admirably to Morris's designs, in which line and pattern were supremely important and shapes needed to be filled smoothly and gracefully. Many of Morris's embroidery designs were worked by professionals employed by his firm, under the direction of Jane. But Morris also produced designs for the Royal School of Needlework and for amateur needlewomen such as Mrs Godman, as well as embroidery kits for such items as cushion covers and fire screens. Deploring the Victorian craze for Berlin wool work (needlepoint), with its garish, overblown floral designs, Morris helped to spearhead the movement to raise the standard of embroidery at both the amateur and the professional level.

Detail

▷ **Wreath** 1876

Wallpaper

WITH ITS RESTRAINED
COLOURING and boldly swirling
forms, this paper is similar in
spirit to *Acanthus* (pages 32-35),
though the luscious poppy
blossoms give it a more frivolous
air. The background patterning is
on a slightly larger scale than in
most Morris designs. Another
difference is that here he has used
solid tone shading on the large
leaves rather than the more
typical lines or dots.

Detail

▷ **Pimpernel** c1876

Wallpaper

THIS SPLENDID DESIGN takes its name from the bright little yellow flowers rather than from the lush old-fashioned poppies that dominate it. The sinuously curving stems anticipate the Art Nouveau style of the later 1800s, without the attenuation characteristic of that style. This complex pattern well illustrates Morris's principles in designing wallpaper: 'You may be as intricate and elaborate in your pattern as you please; nay, the more and more mysteriously you interweave your sprays and stems the better for your purpose, as the whole thing has to be pasted flat on a wall…the fact that we are in this art so little helped by beautiful and varying material (in contrast to designing for textiles) imposes on us the necessity of being especially thoughtful in our designs.'

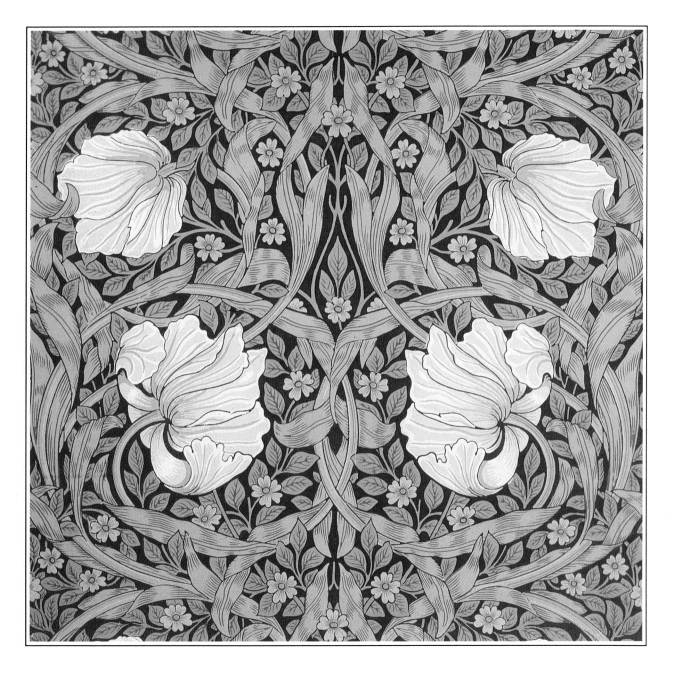

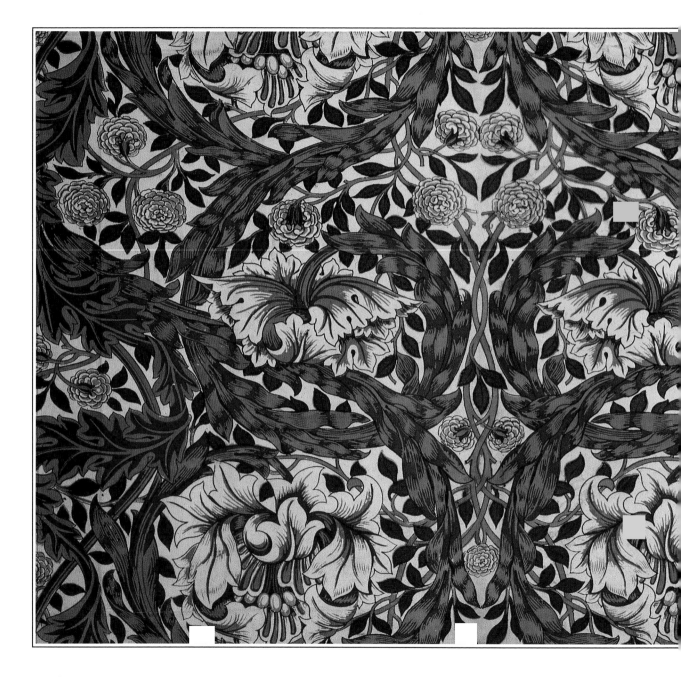

◁ **African Marigold** 1876

Printed fabric

IN THIS DESIGN, ONE OF Morris's boldest designs, the marigolds are thoroughly upstaged by the swirling foliage and lush white blossoms of indeterminate species. The mirror-image horizontal repeat, which Morris used in many of his designs, imposes a measure of control on the exuberant vegetation. The intense blue of the foliage was first obtained at Wardle's plant through the use of Prussian blue, one of the earliest of the chemical dyes. The introduction of these dyes, in the early 1800s, had revolutionized textile printing and dyeing. Cheap and easy to use, they also included colours never before seen – some of them extremely harsh and garish. They also had a tendency to fade, which, happily, sometimes produced an improvement on the original hue. Morris was forced to use these dyes for his early textiles, but he took care to select the deeper and richer shades among them, which faded to an attractive colour.

Detail

▷ **Honeysuckle** 1876

Printed fabric

LIKE *AFRICAN MARIGOLD* (page 49), this richly patterned fabric uses the mirror-pattern repeat that Morris would begin to exploit in his woven textiles in the next few years. It was a very complex structure and a large repeat over the whole width of the fabric. The delicate, circular honeysuckle blossoms (highly appropriate for a wall) gracefully complement the large stylized blooms that dominate the design. *Honeysuckle* was among the first of Morris's fabrics to be printed using natural dyes. This followed several years of experimentation, first at Morris and Co.'s Queen Square premises in London and then at Wardle's dye works. Morris washed the samples and exposed them to sunlight to test their stability, then sent them back to Wardle with detailed comments. The problems of perfecting the colours were exacerbated by a certain printer, whose careless attitude towards matching the colours infuriated Morris: 'It all is a matter of luck how things go…I don't suggest sacking him at once in face of all the present orders, but we can't be for ever under his hippopotamus thumb…'

Detail

Snakeshead 1876

Printed fabric

One of Morris's own favourites among his printed chintzes, *Snakeshead* was inspired partly by imported Indian cotton. It takes its name from the nodding snakeshead fritillary blooms that complement the larger, more formal motifs. It is a superb fusion of drama and control. The assertive flame-like motif and alternating spiky clusters of foliage seem held in suspension by the delicate scrolling blue tendrils that form the background.

Detail

▷ **Rose** 1877

Wallpaper

THIS DESIGN EPITOMIZES Morris's most naturalistic style. One can almost smell the fragrance of the creamy old-fashioned roses on their thorny stems. The veins on the leaves are faithfully drawn, the rose petals carefully distinguished. Yet here, as always, Morris avoided succumbing to *trompe l'oeil* effects. Shading, he insisted, must be used sparingly, for clarity, rather than to try to make an object look round. Here he used lines; in some of his later patterns he chose dots. Inevitably the lines do create an impression of roundness, but only as much as is required to make the blooms 'read' as roses. The background pattern is one of Morris's most subtle. It might be ferns or conifer branches. In places it overlaps the rose stems, strengthening the visual message that all of this growth is in the same plane.

Detail

◁ **Chrysanthemum** 1877

Wallpaper

MORRIS IS SEEN at his most assured in this delightful wallpaper pattern. The basically simple structure of two intertwining stems bearing plump chrysanthemums and (possibly) lilies (the latter owing more than a little to medieval illustrations) is brought to life by Morris's love of natural forms and understanding of how they grow. He insisted that growth in a repeating pattern should be 'rational', advising would-be designers, 'Take heed in this growth that each member of it be strong and crisp, that the lines do not get thready or flabby or too far from their stock to sprout firmly and vigorously…'

Detail

▷ **Bower** 1877

Wallpaper

A LIVELY, LUXURIANT DESIGN, *Bower* is a fine example both of Morris's sympathetic treatment of natural forms and of his mastery of structure. The two main motifs alternate rhythmically, with the small peach-coloured flowers and the busy background of feathery little leaves (reminiscent of Chinese painting) providing a smooth transition between them. One of Morris's goals as a designer of wallpapers was to conceal the construction of the pattern 'enough to prevent people from counting repeats'. In *Bower* this seamless quality has been achieved in a most graceful manner.

Detail

▷ **Bird** 1878

Woven fabric

ONE OF FOUR WOVEN TEXTILES featuring pairs of birds that Morris designed in the late 1870s, this elaborate, formal fabric was originally woven as hangings for the drawing room of Kelmscott House, Hammersmith, Morris's London home for the last 18 years of his life. He drew his inspiration for it from woven silks from Italy, which he believed to be medieval. *Bird* was woven in wool as a double cloth – that is, a two-layer, reversible fabric formed from two warps and two wefts which are interchanged across the pattern, thus holding the two layers together. The alternating pairs of birds, with wings folded and spread, facing and turned away from each other, form a lively counterpoint to the intricately structured background.

Detail

◁ **Cabbage and Vine** 1879

Tapestry

THIS ELABORATELY PATTERNED
hanging was Morris's first attempt
at tapestry! He produced it
between May and September
1879, having learned the
technique from a book and
working on a loom he had set up
in his bedroom in Kelmscott
House. Originally called *Acanthus
and Vine*, it acquired its more
familiar name because of the
exuberant round shapes created by
the somewhat undisciplined
acanthus leaves. Morris had a high
regard for tapestry, which he called
'the noblest of the weaving arts'. In
this technique the design is created
entirely by the weft threads, each
thread being combed down on to
the one below, covering the warp
completely. Many tapestries were
produced by Morris and Co. from
1881 onwards at their new
premises at Merton Abbey, Surrey.
They often depicted figures from
classical or Arthurian mythology
drawn by Burne-Jones, shown
against a profusion of foliage and
flowers designed by Morris.

▷ **Evenlode** 1883

Printed fabric

IN 1881 MORRIS AND CO. acquired the Merton Abbey works in Surrey, where *Evenlode* was one of the first fabrics to be printed. The premises had previously been used by calico printers and so needed relatively little alteration. Most important, they were situated on the river Wandle, whose soft water was well suited to the dyeing process. Here, at last, Morris began to do his own printing, employing, where appropriate, the indigo discharge method, which enabled him to produce complex designs using his favourite rich blue. It was a lengthy process. First the cloth was dyed blue in the indigo vat, then block printed with a bleach on all areas not intended to be blue or to contain blue (such as violet). Where a light blue was required, as for the leaves in *Evenlode*, a dilute bleaching solution was applied separately, the cloth was then washed to remove the excess blue. Subsequent primary colours were added by printing those areas with a mordant (fixing agent) and then immersing the fabric in the dye; any areas not mordanted would not take the dye.

◁ **Wey** 1883

Printed fabric

LIKE *EVENLODE* (page 63), this design was named for a river not far from Merton Abbey, and its diagonally wandering stems – even more than the swaying ones in *Evenlode* – do suggest the flow of water. Here again, Morris exploited the indigo discharge method to produce a deep blue ground. Wey was used not only for a chintz but also for velveteen. Printed velveteens were very popular in the 1880s, and Morris and Co. catered for this fashion by offering a few designs on velveteen, although the special finishing required for this fabric made its production somewhat onerous.

▷ **Cray** 1884

Printed fabric

To PRINT COMPLEX PATTERNS many blocks would be required, not only for different colours but for different areas of the design, as a typical block measured only about 20–25 cm (8–10 in) square. This large-scale design with a vertical repeat of 92 cm (36¼ in) is the most complex of all Morris's printed textiles, requiring 34 blocks, and was consequently the most expensive. Its strongly diagonal character was inspired by a 17th century Italian cut velvet that had caught Morris's eye in the South Kensington Museum in 1883. The boldness of the design is enhanced by Morris's favourite blue and red palette, the dark blue background accentuating the meandering stems. In another colourway, using peach tones for the flowers and a grey-green background, the design takes on a more restful aspect.

△ **Lodden** 1884

Printed fabric

'I DON'T SUPPOSE we shall get many people to buy them,' wrote Morris disconsolately of his printed fabrics in 1875, when they were still selling slowly. Within a few years, however, his determination began to pay off, and Morris and Co. chintzes and other printed furnishing fabrics became a great success. *Lodden*, which was printed on a cotton and linen blend, is still being produced (by Liberty & Co.), along with many other Morris designs (mainly by Sanderson's). It is one of the most fresh and charming of all Morris's textile designs, and is especially attractive in this clear, bright colourway. As ingenious as an Elizabethan knot garden, it manages to be both dense and light at the same time.

△ **Lea** 1885

Printed fabric

IN THIS INTRIGUINGLY
CONVOLUTED design there is no
dominant image but, rather, an
interplay of swirling leaves
(anticipating those in Morris's
Wallflower wallpaper design of
1890 (page 72) and assorted small
blossoms, which seem at first to
belong to the background but
which overlap the large leaves in
various places. This overlapping
serves to reinforce the flatness of
the pattern, and the almost equal
emphasis given to the positive and
negative shapes gives the design a
'yin-yang' quality.

◁ **Medway** 1885

Printed fabric

THIS CHARMING, SIMPLE DESIGN forms a striking contrast to the complex *Lea* (page 67), produced in the same year. The inspiration for the meandering stem was the same cut velvet that Morris drew on for *Cray* (page 65) and several other designs. The effect here is fresh and unselfconscious. The design (later adapted for a wallpaper called *Garden Tulip*) seems to evoke the spirit of Merton Abbey itself, which was described in 1886 by an American visitor in admiring words: 'scrupulous neatness and order reigned everywhere…pleasant smells of dried herbs…blent with the wholesome odors of grass and flowers and sunny summer warmth that freely circulated through open doors and windows.' This visitor had the good fortune not only to choose an atypically warm summer day but evidently also to miss the stage at which indigo dye is ready for dipping, when its smell resembles, according to another visitor, 'stinking meat roasted'.

▷ **Redcar Carpet** c1881–5

Original design

MORRIS'S ENTHUSIASM FOR HAND-KNOTTED carpets dates from the late 1850s, when he began buying oriental carpets as furnishings for Red House. But however much he admired the profusion of abstract shapes typical of these, he insisted that carpets produced in Europe should have their own distinctive style: 'I, as a Western man and picture lover…must have unmistakable suggestions of gardens and fields and strange trees, boughs and tendrils.'

This original watercolour design for the Redcar carpet (showing a quarter of the pattern), with its lush blooms, illustrates this aesthetic. The soft colouring was used for the actual carpet. The striking border complements the design of the main pattern, setting up its own lively, undulating rhythm.

◁ **Woodpecker** 1885

Tapestry

THIS IS ONE OF THE VERY FEW tapestries designed entirely by Morris, another being *Cabbage and Vine* (page 62). Characteristically, it shows a greater interest in pattern than in the ostensible subject, with Morris's cherished acanthus leaves somewhat encroaching upon the fruit tree with its feathered occupants. The top and bottom borders of the tapestry bear the legend ' I once a king and chief, now am the tree-bark's thief, ever twist trunk and leaf, chasing the prey.' In the side borders, honeysuckle vines bearing delicate flower clusters climb up trellis poles.

▷ **Net Ceiling**

Ceiling paper

EARLY CEILING PAPERS consisted simply of rosettes, intended to suggest plaster work in the centre of a ceiling, from which a chandelier would be hung. Later they covered the whole area. A directional design was obviously inappropriate here, and in his designs for ceiling paper Morris used a completely different style than those he used for walls. Here are light, open, highly stylized shapes in medallion configurations, usually in one colour on a white or cream ground. This one is somewhat more elaborate, and would have completed the decoration of a grand room in a suitably luxurious manner.

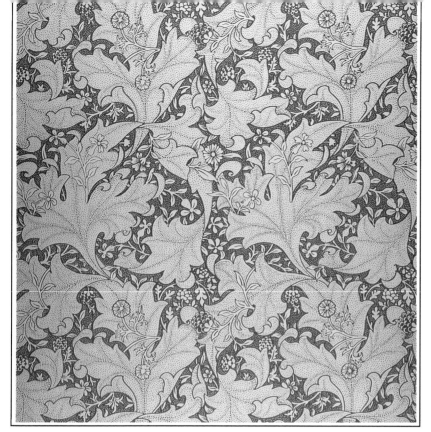

△ **Wallflower** 1890

Wallpaper

WITH HIS DISLIKE of 18th century styles, Morris would not have been pleased to hear this design described as 'rococo'. Yet it does have some of the playful quality of that style, even if its merrily swirling leaves are kept under control by the discipline of the repeat. Here Morris uses finely speckled dots for the shading, rather than the lines used in earlier patterns; even the veins of the leaves are rendered in this way. The blue background is given softness and depth through the use of a beaded texture.

▷ **Pink and Rose** c1890

Wallpaper

LIKE *WALLFLOWER* (left), its near contemporary, this design employs only two colours, perhaps to cater for the growing taste for lightness and simplicity in interior design at this period. The mainly vertical structure of this pattern is much more straightforward than the intricate meanderings of *Pimpernel* (page 46), for example, or the sculptural subtleties of *Acanthus* (pages 32–35). The representation of the flowers recalls some of the conventions of 17th century crewel embroidery, then enjoying a revival (thanks in part to Morris himself). A touch of exoticism typical of crewel work is provided by the spiky-petalled blossoms that alternate with the more familiar pinks and Tudor roses.

◁ **Willow Bough** 1887

Wallpaper (fabric 1895)

THE PERFECT SIMPLICITY of this design typifies the lighter, clearer look becoming fashionable for interiors in the late 1800s. It is the ideal complement to the Queen Anne style of architecture, with its restrained red brick facades and crisp white trim, or to the later 'prairie houses' of Frank Lloyd Wright. Having previously demonstrated his virtuosity in handling complex structures in such designs as *Pimpernel* (page 46), *Lodden* (page 66) and *Cray* (page 65), Morris here shows what can be achieved with the simplest of means by someone with a complete mastery of line.

▷ **Bullerswood** 1889

Hand-knotted carpet

THIS SPLENDID CARPET was a collaboration between Morris and his assistant John Henry Dearle, who, after Morris's death, became the company's art director. Dearle's hand can be seen in the crisply delineated branches that meander through the design, Morris's in the colouring and in the pairs of birds that perch in the branches. The carpet is very large: 7.4 x 3.9 m (24 ft 3 in x 12 ft 10 in). Such carpets were, of course, very expensive, and throughout his working life Morris deplored the fact that most of his work was accessible only to the rich, or at least the relatively prosperous. A client once found him pacing and muttering angrily to himself, and when he asked what the matter was received the tactless reply, 'It's only that I spend my life in ministering to the swinish luxury of the rich!' Then, as now, artistry and fine craftsmanship cost money. However, Morris and Co. did produce designs for machine-made carpets, which were woven by various firms, and were considerably less expensive than hand-knotted ones.

◁ **'Aesthetic' Interior**

THIS DISPLAY OF FURNISHINGS from the late 19th century includes works by William Morris – the chairs and the *Peacock and Dragon* hangings – and by William de Morgan, a pottery designer who worked for a while with Morris at Merton Abbey. He was a leading figure in the Arts and Crafts movement, famous especially for his tiles. Like Morris, he eschewed three-dimensional effects in his work, preferring to exploit the possibilities of flat pattern. Much of his inspiration came from Greece and Persia. The exotic quality of much of his work, and of such Morris textiles as *Peacock and Dragon*, were appreciated by the so-called Aesthetic Movement, which favoured highly decorative furnishings, especially in oriental styles, and rather spindly furniture, such as this sideboard and corner cabinet.

▽ **Blackthorn** c1892

Wallpaper (possibly by J.H. Dearle)

THE SHARPLY DEFINED FLOWERS and foliage of this design, previously thought to be by Morris, are highly characteristic of Dearle, whose work it may be. The clear, bright colours against the dark background are slightly reminiscent of medieval *mille-fleurs* tapestries. Dearle first entered Morris's employ in 1878 as an assistant in the company's shop in Oxford Street, London, where he learned some of the techniques employed by the firm, including glass painting and tapestry weaving. He showed a natural artistic aptitude, and under Morris's tutelage went on to design textiles, including embroidery, and wallpapers. Another well-known Morris and Co. design, *Compton*, which was used for both printed cotton and wallpaper, is now known to have been designed by Dearle.

◁ **Honeysuckle** 1883

(possibly by May Morris)

THIS ENCHANTING DESIGN is believed to be by Morris's younger daughter, May (1862-1939). If so, it clearly shows that she inherited her father's sensitivity to nature. The blossoms are wonderfully lifelike, and in this softly glowing colourway, with its duck-egg blue ground, they seem to conjure up a warm summer's day. The freely flowing pattern enhances the naturalistic effect. Morris encouraged both his daughters to take an active interest in his work – for example, giving them, as children, samples of yarn for experimenting with vegetable dyes. May showed a special talent for textile design, and after attending the South Kensington School of Design, she began working for her father, overseeing the embroidery department. She designed many large-scale embroideries for the firm and published many articles and a book on the craft. Among her other contributions as a designer were some bindings for the Kelmscott Press.

ACKNOWLEDGEMENTS

The Publisher would like to thank the following for their kind permission to reproduce the paintings in this book:

Bridgeman Art Library, London /Tate Gallery, London: 8-9; **/Victoria & Albert Museum, London:** Cover, Half-title, 10-19, 28-35, 38-51, 54-61, 64-65, 67, 72-74, 77-78; **/Kelmscott Manor, Oxfordshire:** 20-21, 62; **/Photo: Ann S. Dean, Malvern:** 24-25; **/Bonhams, London:** 26; **/Church of St Michael, Waterford, Herts:** 27; **/Photo: John Bethell:** 63, 68; **/William Morris Gallery, Walthamstow, London:** 70; **/The Fine Art Society, London:** 76-77; **William Morris Gallery, Walthamstow, London:** 36-37, 52-53; **Courtesy of the Trustees of the Victoria & Albert Museum, London:** 22-23, 66, 69, 71, 75